KAYNEISMS OF INSPIRATION

By

OMEGA KAYNE

OMEGA KAYNE MEDIA

P.O. BOX 250432

ATLANTA, GA 30325

OMEGA@OMEGAKAYNE.COM

Copyright © 2013 by Omega Kayne

ISBN-13: 978-0989185134

ISBN-10: 0989185133

Manufactured in the United States

DEDICATION

To my healthy and happy son: You don't know how
much you have inspired your father to do the things that
I hope will one day make you proud to say, "That's MY
dad!" When you were introduced to the world, your
mother and I knew we had a special PRINCE that JAH
blessed us with and you have been a GIFT to us both
since day one. I live for the moments when I hear you
call out, "DADDY", as that word is the sweetest and most
comforting word that a dad could ever hear. NOTHING
else matters in my world but you, your well-being and
your happiness. All of this will make sense to you when
you become older, but for now I will continue to spread
my LOVE for you all over the Planet and leave a legacy
for you so that you will have CHOICES in this world. You
will ALWAYS know that your FATHER expressed his
LOVE for you every chance he had. Every Quote,
Thought and Inspirational Phrase that will be in this
book will have a direct correlation to how I will
consistently live and teach you to someday share your
fathers experiences with your children. You have been
the only TRUE example of unconditional LOVE that I
have ever received because you have no clue at this
moment in your very young life what Judgments,
Expectations, Ridicules, Failures and Untruths are so
everything you are giving the world is in its purest form,
and I accept it with gratitude. JAH, gave me the

GREATEST GIFT in a Son that is you and I will HONOR you in Life and in Spirit, my Prince. I will FOREVER be YOUR FATHER as you will ALWAYS and FOREVER be my little baby boy!

The King to His Prince......

Acknowledgements

Any person's walk in life will be attached to someone who helped shape the person they are attempting to become as each day we change and grow. There have been hundreds of inspiring things and people who have shaped me and, in some form or fashion, I have personally acknowledged you because I know for a fact I couldn't have done it by myself. It is only right that I acknowledge my family, friends and home community of **St. Petersburg, Florida** for all the support you have shown me throughout the years. I acknowledge the city of **Lafayette**, as well as the entire state of **Louisiana**, for showing a city boy some good, old-fashioned, country love and, most especially, for introducing me to my **BROTHERS** in the Fold: **WE ARE GAMMA DELTA** and I hope I'm making you proud. To my **Los Angeles, California family:** I LOVE the WEST and you have introduced me to the place where LAID BACK is truly LAID BACK. I needed YOU over 20 years ago and you welcomed me with open arms. **Tyrone Tann**, my Filipino brother from another mother and the **FIRST** guy to show me the ropes in HOLLYWOOD: We have made history and made many movies together, my writing and producing partner, but your friendship goes beyond

5

ANYTHING that could measure as your SPIRIT can be felt by ALL who come in contact with you. And, where would I be if it had not been for the **QUEEN** who gave me life? **I LOVE YOU, MOM**. The many sacrifices you've made to provide for me and my brother will **NEVER** be in vain. As I climb, we climb; and, I will keep my part in the promise to RETIRE you so that you can finally ENJOY LIFE. JAH knows the heart and why it beats, and each one has your name on it. **YOUR SONS** will make a way out of NO WAY so you can smell the roses NOW. **M. Mattox**, there are NO WORDS that can be written to explain the admiration I have for you my friend. THANK YOU for the LIFE JACKET. Because of you, NEVER will I sink and I thank you a million times over. **J. Nixon**: Your friendship and conversations have helped me in ways, brother, that are not seen in many men. You have said that I've helped you, but your help TOWERS mine. JAH made another LION in you. And last but not least, my editor, **Stephanie "Cookie" Armelin**, you are making this "BOOK THING" a pleasure. I'm glad our friendship has sustained 20 years and that we are basking in these good moments together. THANK YOU A MILLY and JAH bless you and the spirit that is YOU!

steph.the.editor1913@gmail.com

Introduction

"Kayneisms of Inspiration" is a collection of my own
personal quotes and inspirations that I have created at
different points in my life when times were hard, fun,
happy: the life lessons and the "a-ha" moments. This
book is not only meant to inspire, but it is also intended
to be a guideline for your life's situations. You can apply
each quote to your life and tailor it so that you can
someday pay it forward to help someone else who may
need to be encouraged or inspired. By no means do I
have all the answers to all the problems in the world.
I'm only a vessel navigating through life and still
learning to ride its waves; but, I've found a special gift
inside me that is able to turn thoughts into words and
release them out into the world. This gift has helped
those who have listened and I felt a need to share this
with the world; and, if I am able to help one more person
SEE IT THROUGH, then this creation will be well worth
its weight in knowledge. This book of "Kayneisms" will
consist of many quotes that I've created and applied to
my very own life. I will first explain how each applies to
me. On the opposite, blank pages, you will then apply
each quote to your life and write how it can help you
and help others. This book is intended to be part
inspiration and part journal. At its end, you will have
written your own *"isms"* of inspiration that you can share

with the world. Everyone should have an inspiration to share.

These are mine…

TABLE OF CONTENTS

"When I was a child, I was told I could be ANYTHING I wanted to be…and I believed it."

I was very blessed in the sense that I had some very influential people in my life that saw my potential and made it their business to always remind me that there was *favor* placed upon me. Of course, as a young boy I had no clue what favor meant nor did I understand why everyone I came in contact with would have the same sentiment, but I quickly learned that people see things in you that you most likely won't see in yourself.

I wasn't born from money. I lived in some unforgiving places and did many unforgivable things that I still thank the Most High for sparing me from. But, I guess that was the *favor* that many associated with me. I knew I wanted to be someone who everyone could remember and be proud of so I made sure I made the grades, stayed out of harm's way and believed there was a world outside of the box we as humans are born into. I **never** wanted to be like the masses; different was **always** the road I chose and because of that I sought out things that were hard to achieve. For me, the challenge was in the lesson of how far I could go when obstacles were many. Twenty-plus years later, I have a pretty lengthy resume' and it was all because **I BELIEVED I WAS SUPPOSED TO BE HERE**!!

APPLY TO YOUR LIFE... WRITE IT DOWN AND LIVE

"Every day remind YOURSELF that NOBODY owes you ANYTHING and your DREAMS are NOT EVERYONE else's DREAMS."

By far this will be one of your highest hurdles to jump because in some form or fashion we all seek VALIDATION from those we love and those who love us but it is a FACT that those who genuinely love you may NOT share your drive, commitment, tenacity and passion for what YOU believe in.

When I chose to go into the entertainment business I had many tell me to go ahead and pursue it because they knew my drive, but I had many more ask me was I sure I wanted go into that field because not everyone makes it. I NEVER LISTENED TO THOSE WHO QUESTIONED MY DECISION and did what I felt was best for me. If I succeeded it would be because I wasn't a good listener when it came to those who were DREAM STEALERS.

Yes, you will encounter dream stealers, dream downers and wet blankets who will do everything in their power to steer you in the path they WERE NEVER BOLD ENOUGH TO FOLLOW. For them, it would be much easier to talk you out of your dreams than to encourage you to keep walking to a place they never envisioned visiting. Friends, family, spouses and parents will be the culprits in many cases and it's a shame, but the GREAT thing about life is that YOU have a CHOICE. My choice was to NEVER allow my future to be dictated by someone else's interpretation for my future…and I NEVER will!

APPLY TO YOUR LIFE.....WRITE IT DOWN AND LIVE

"When you have told all the lies, played all the games and done all the damage, you still have to live with yourself."

I have definitely been guilty of this, as there was a time in my life where I suffered from the *"fake it 'til you make it" syndrome*. In my case, I tasted success throughout my early life and that was all that was associated with me, but the reality of it all was this: not all of my days were good.

I've had many disappointments and failures. I've had times where I've had a lot of money and more times I've been broke, but my PRIDE wouldn't allow me to show that discontent that I was indeed living. It was too embarrassing. What would my friends and family say? Why give the people who I knew were rooting against me the satisfaction of knowing I was failing?

I've played games with the emotions of those who meant well for me and I did this because it was undetectable and I could get away with it. I wasn't concerned about the damage I was doing to others. I was more concerned with what I could get out of it for me. SELFISHNESS fueled my desires and caused a lot of damage to those who were willing to share with me. All I wanted to do was take.

Until I realized that PROVING needed to be removed from my MACHISMO demeanor, I was constantly digging myself into a hole that was getting harder to pull myself out of. When this is the case, your EGO is the one who gets the last laugh.

The TRUTH of Karma has visited me many times and the fact of the matter is that it was HARD living the lie of something I COULD NO LONGER keep up. It took years to figure this out and, when I did, I became a happier person and truly began to love the skin I was in.

APPLY TO YOUR LIFE....... WRITE IT DOWN AND LIVE

"Life will never make sense if you keep questioning what it's trying to teach you."

I don't know anyone who has had a trial or tribulation and haven't asked themselves, "Why?" It's hard not to. You try to be a good person. You do all the right things. You're helpful but you still find yourself in between a rock and a hard place and you have no clue why. We all can be selfish at times. As humans, we fail to see the lesson being taught when things may not be going our way, so we focus on the problem at hand.

Yes, I know this all too well as I'm still dealing with the "*whys*" in difficulty but I also know the "Why ME?" is not as important as the "Why NOW?" Lessons will not always be visible, tangible or obvious. There will be some lessons that you will have to seek actively in order for it to make sense within the spectrum of your issue.

Life is the greatest gift that any of us can be given; it's our problems that give life the bad rap. I have been told, "Bad times don't last forever." We all NEED to believe in that because once your LESSON is learned for life's TEST, there will be brighter days ahead…but always be ready for the next storm.

Yes, life has revolving doors. So don't waste your time trying to figure of WHY bad things happen. Concentrate on HOW you can overcome your difficulties and make

your life better for that moment in time. ENJOY the LIFE
that you have been blessed with because you cannot
change what is destined to be. Make sure you spread this
thought to younger generations so that we can attempt to
create a more harmonious society. When they are met
with adversities, they will not think that it's the end of
the world. It may just be the beginning of the new things
the WORLD is trying to show them and the new
direction they need to go.

APPLY TO YOUR LIFE......WRITE IT DOWN AND LIVE

"The day I realized there was no ceiling on what I could accomplish was the day I became the CEO of ME."

I don't believe I was ever cut out for a regular job. I know that I may have been qualified to do many things but I just knew that once you reached a certain level that was it. I also didn't like the fact that someone else had control over when my time could be over in a place of business. There's something unfulfilling about being at the mercy of someone else and I never wanted to depend on that mercy for my well-being, so I decided to be my own CEO.

Having control over your own destiny can be the most fulfilling thing that anyone could ever imagine but it's also the most risky. I've never been afraid to take risks because I knew I was a good "product." I always believed that if I put my mind to something I would create the same interest or cause the same effect that any corporate tycoon could and reap all the rewards.

When I began acting, I was only concerned about being in front of the camera. I thought the sensation of that exhilaration I felt from that was enough until I started paying attention to, and asking questions about, the other roles that were played within the Hollywood machine. I came to find out that the producers and writers make the most money on a project. The actors serve only as the visual manifestation of the work. Once the actors get

23

paid for their services, the financial compensation for all of their hard work is done. But, if you position yourself as one of the major "players" of a project, (i.e., producer, writer, etc.) then you can negotiate points on the back end which entitles you to more revenue…the kind of revenue that keeps paying you years and years after the initial project has been completed.

BINGO!!! The ceiling opened up for me once I learned the laws of the land. Control is everything and when you learn your true value, you will never want a ceiling above you again. It's time for you to fire your inner employee and become the CEO of your own life.

APPLY TO YOUR LIFE…..WRITE IT DOWN AND LIVE

"Who gives a Sh** what others may think of you? Carry on with your life anyway!"

I believe that all of us deal with wanting to make others happy and have others approve of our life's choices. By nature, we are pleasers because we have been reared to be. For many years I was a pleaser. There is nothing wrong with that if that is who you are, but there will come a time in life when pleasing yourself will become essential to your own happiness and you'll be forced to choose between your own well-being and someone else's.

I've come to realize that no matter how much good someone does in life there will be folks who are unappreciative of those good efforts and will still treat you like you have done them wrong or, worse yet, like what you have done is not enough. So I decided a long time ago to just remove the "need-to-please" component from my good intentions and learned to just be satisfied with my efforts and accept the fact that nobody will be a bigger cheerleader for me than I am.

It would be great if your peers could acknowledge you when you do well, but in the real world, that probably won't happen. You sometimes have to accept the fact that when we deal with other people, we will be met with conditional acceptance and there is simply no way to avoid that. Your life must move on whether you receive the pat on the back from others or not. But, if you learn how to stretch your arm a bit longer you'll probably be able to get that same pat by doing it yourself.

APPLY TO YOUR LIFE........WRITE IT DOWN AND LIVE

"When your need to succeed outweighs your fear of failure, you will finally be able to take flight!"

The greatest thing about achievement is that we are ALL born with the same thing…the "it's possible" gene!!! With anything, any desire and any thought, it will always start with the most important ingredient: faith. TAKE THAT STEP! The first step will ALWAYS be the hardest, but it is the most crucial one because, without it, all dreams and aspirations lay dormant!

As long as I've known that I wanted to be successful I've known I had to go out on a limb and take chances. Yes, fear lives in all of us but how do you use yours? I LOVE FEAR!!! I've found a sure-fire way to use the scariest word known to man to my advantage; and it has helped me climb mountains, swim in deep waters and see the sun through stormy weather. I keep fear within arm's reach but ALWAYS behind me. Why behind me, you may ask? As long as fear is behind me, it will always have to catch up for me to acknowledge it exists. As long as I stay in front of it, it can NEVER put up barricades between me and my next achievement.

I acknowledge that fear has its place. I don't think I'll ever not want it or need it in my life because fear keeps me honest and motivated. Any time I may question myself or my abilities I just look over my shoulder to see fear there waiting for me. Now, I can slow down and give "fear" the chance to touch me on the shoulder or I can keep moving forward to keep distance between it and me. I choose the latter. Every day I look over my shoulder just to say, "Are you ready? It's a new day and I have new goals to accomplish! LET'S GO!"

APPLY TO YOUR LIFE........ WRITE IT DOWN AND LIVE

"If you aggressively engage in keeping your standards high, then subpar expectations can never manifest themselves in your life!"

It's never too late to do this! Some of us don't get this until we've gone through some difficult things and have a bar to measure how hard we have to work to reach our greatest heights. I never shot below my bar of expectations but I most certainly was happy and accepted the fact that I was able to meet those expectations head on. It wasn't until I was older that I realized I wasn't challenging myself and, if I was happy with just meeting my expectations, then how was I to know when I was truly being tested?

From that point on I decided that I deserved to accept and respond to a higher desire and expectation for myself. Too many times we become comfortable with doing "just enough" because we start to believe that having low expectation is OK- its average-but what if ALL OF US decided AVERAGE was subpar and we would NEVER PLANT any of our most precious seeds in infertile soil? Our collective mindset needs to change when it comes to this, whether it be in love, life, relationships, jobs or personal reflections. I've gotten so used to this way of life that when I THINK I'm about to shoot below the bar my gauge kicks in and says to me, "What the heck are you doing? YOU ARE BETTER THAN THAT!"

There is NOTHING wrong with feeling and KNOWING that you are the prize, but you have to back it up with actions that show YOU BELIEVE everything that you're about makes you valuable. DON'T WAIT for someone else to raise the bar for you. BE PROACTIVE and raise it YOURSELF!

"Some people wait for success to happen. I sprint to it to wake its ass up!"

If this is you, then this is a Kayneism you really need to pay attention to! Nothing will ever happen for you if you WAIT for it to happen. Most successful people are the ones who have gone out on a limb expecting "NO" but found "YES!" This wouldn't have happened if they'd just sat and waited.

You have to go out and make a way out of no way. Expect the "no's" but accept the "yeses" when they come. If an idea doesn't work immediately, it doesn't mean that it's NEVER going to work. It just means that it won't work right now.

Don't disregard your "no's." Trust me, I'm a living witness; they do turn into "yeses" eventually, but you have to keep fighting. I was once a major player in the waiting game because I believed that the universe would open up and just give me all of her precious pearls. Being broke quickly changed that philosophy. I realized that nobody will just give you what you think you deserve out of life!

So I said, "I need to be more proactive in guiding my own ship. I'm qualified to be a captain so stop thinking like a deckhand." Too many of us are deckhands on someone else's ship but truly have captain aspirations. I've been guiding my own ship for the past twenty-five years. The freedom you receive from this gives you a sense of accomplishment because off of your own merit you made a way.

In many cases, people can be very selfish when it comes to helping you to get where you want to be. That doesn't make them wrong. It makes you wrong for getting upset that you're relying on someone else's boot straps to pull yourself up. Rely on your own ingenuity first and if someone else is gracious enough to assist you in your walk always bring something that you can cook to the table!

APPLY TO YOUR LIFE........WRITE IT DOWN AND LIVE

"Let go of those who refuse to be held by you!"

The hardest lesson about this Kayneism is not wanting to let go of something or someone that you know is not good for you. Maybe it's because of the security of familiarity. Maybe it's the comfort zone that we have become used to, but the lines are surely blurred when it's time to become unattached. I have been in this situation a few times in my life because I'm loyal, sometimes to a fault.

Genuinely, I try to make things work. I apologize even when I know someone else is at fault. I keep calm so that my composure can be infectious to those I'm around, but I had to learn that some people are just not meant for you and you are not meant for them. Yes, this will hurt like hell to walk away from something or someone you think is tailor-made for you, but don't be so blinded to the lesson that may be attempting to surface right in front of your very eyes. If they are refusing you and your inner-voice is sending you warning signals, you must take heed to what the universe is trying to convey. Don't ignore that instinct because it's there for a reason.

We shouldn't have to force someone to care for us, to love us, to have our best interests at heart. Allow them to do you a favor and exit stage left. Tears will follow. Your heart will cry. You will fight what is good for you; but,

when you decide that you are finished strolling in the
storm then you can finally decide to run in the sun!

APPLY TO YOUR LIFE........WRITE IT DOWN AND LIVE

" Hardship is ALWAYS accompanied by sacrifice!"

Wow! I can speak on this for hours, and I'm sure you can, too. Most of us have dealt with hardships in life that will either build our character or completely tear us down. The truth of this is SACRIFICE is akin to HARDSHIP!

I, like millions of others, have had to sacrifice to get something better in life. Many times we cannot see the prize immediately because the hardships keep a cloak on our vision. Those hardships have challenged me daily. I've wanted to quit and give up on what I was attempting to accomplish and delve into something more rational or that would make more sense.

Honestly, I tried this and one thing I found out was I CANNOT FOOL MYSELF! So I continue to sacrifice through all the hurt and pain because the big picture is the end result and the reward will make sense to ME. Many tears and much heartache accompany hardship but the reward of enduring those hardships brings the sunshine and smiles that make it all worth it.

How far are you willing to go for your sunshine? I am willing to risk drowning in a torrential storm to get what I feel is meant for me. So, if I have to tread the rough waters to test my endurance, then that's what I'll do. There are hundreds of things I'd much rather be doing but there are only a few things that I definitely want to do. I suggest you endure and find what makes you happy because if you don't, you will have plenty of regretful mornings as you head to a job you detest.

APPLY TO YOUR LIFE.........WRITE IT DOWN AND LIVE

"When silence is the loudest thing you hear, sit still and listen to what it has to say!"

I have learned so many lessons from just sitting still and shutting my mouth! It is not always good to be the loudest person in the room as most who take on this personality trait usually have nothing of importance to say.

The majority of my life-changing moments have come to fruition because I silenced myself and listened to what the universe was trying to tell me. So many times we think we have all the answers. Clearly, we don't because we are always asking the Most High for guidance and answers; but, almost 9.9 out of 10 times we ignore what He's trying to tell us.

Why are we hard-headed? Why don't we listen? Heck, why don't we take our own advice as opposed to always trying to give it to someone else? It's because we DON'T live the creed of having FAITH.

One of our biggest problems is that we allow the loudness of self-ridicule to drown out God's messages to us. There will be many times that you will have to have honest conversations with yourself and allow truth to speak to you; and, the only way you can do this is to be silent and accept whatever avenues that the Most High is trying to lead you to. Be silent! Stop fighting against the current and just go with the flow. You might just be amazed at the places you can go!

" You can't deceive FATE no matter how much you try!"

You can be the fastest runner in the world. You can be
the biggest con artist and the best magician in the show
but one thing you can never be is a deceiver of fate! We
may want to believe that we are much smarter than we
truly are but Fate will always be smarter and craftier.
What is meant to be will be; and there is no way to avoid
just HOW things will be.

I realized this to be true while in my mid-thirties. On my
life's voyage, I would become so frustrated with trying to
change my course by attempting to manipulate the
"sails." Every time I'd try to steer, my ship would go
exactly where **it** wanted to go instead of where I was
trying to lead it. Do you know why? Because it was my
destiny to endure the rough waves of life and no matter
how much I tried to fight and steer toward calmer
waters, my journey was fated to be a complicated one.
These hardships taught me valuable lessons about
patience, too, because at any given time the winds of life
can change your direction.

When I wished for paved roads, dirt roads were all I had
to travel. Sure, I'd ask JAH, "Why me? Why can't I have it
easier?" Trust me I waited to hear the answers to these
questions but soon gave in to the fact that my purpose
was already pre –destined and what I had to do was just
hold on because the sharp turns were going to happen.

The hills were going to be steep. There would be unexpected attacks on this journey but if I remained steadfast, eventually I would be led to a calm plain and it would all make sense.

Sometimes, I still ask, "Why me," because Fate still determines my journey but I've come to grips with the fact that this path is mine alone and it is purposeful. It's meant to teach me lessons about this world and about myself. Make it your goal to find your life's purpose in your FATEFUL walk and know that you must endure whatever hardships may come in order to fulfill that purpose.

APPLY TO YOUR LIFE........ WRITE IT DOWN AND LIVE

"Stop waiting for people to SEE who you are and start showing them!"

After being in the entertainment industry for more than twenty years, I know all too well how we sometimes wait to be "discovered" by someone. We attempt to be in the right place at the right time and to say all the right things. Then, there are those who sit back and remain silent, expecting their lives to change just because they believe they deserve a chance.

Unfortunately, that's not how real life works. You have to be proactive with everything that you do because nothing is just going to fall into your lap. For as long as I can remember I have always gone the route of trying to make things happen the way I wanted them to as opposed to waiting for *something* to happen. I knew I had a lot to offer and if nobody else noticed, it was my job to bring them to my reality

Some will take that bodacious attitude as being arrogant, cocky, or even self-serving. This all may be true, but ask yourself this: "Are those same folks that judge you waiting to be noticed or heard? Are they standing in the way of the very successes that may be awaiting *them* if they would just open their mouths to be heard or got up off their asses and did something new and different?"

The big question here is, "What are you waiting for?" No matter who you are, you're great and talented and the world needs to know this about you. More than half of my successes have come from me believing that nobody knew anything about the real me and I needed to change that. I have this saying, "They may not have come to see me, but when they leave, they'll be asking who the hell I am!"

APPLY TO YOUR LIFE........ WRITE IT DOWN AND LIVE

"Be bold enough to tell No, 'NO!'"

If you always bow down when someone tells you NO, you will never be successful at anything! I say this with total conviction. You will sometimes have to show doubtful people that they are wrong about you or whatever you are attempting to persuade them to believe in.

I can't imagine any of our greatest inventors and achievers taking their first 'no' and throwing away their blueprint. You should always get second, third and sometimes fourth opinions, as well as look into other options and ways to see your visions through.

I've stopped counting the "no's" I've heard over the course of my life because holding on to rejection gets in the way of success. I find ways to accept every 'no' as a temporary answer and, in my mind, turn them into "maybes' and 'not yets.' Hell, I sometimes turn them into premature "yeses" because I believe that "no" will never be MY final answer.

You have to be bold and aggressive in life, period. Nobody owes you anything and, the last time I checked, nobody was giving away anything free and easily. You've heard the adage, "Nothing worth having comes easy." It's true and I can attest to that. Although to some it may seem that it has been a very easy road for me, I've learned to make how I handle my struggles look effortless. Others only see the finished performance but have no clue what the dress rehearsal is like!

So, don't allow 'no' to be the ending of your continuous progress toward whatever you choose to do. Know from the start that you will hear it more than you want to, but no matter how many times you hear it, just keep on pushing and eventually someone is going to say, "YES!"

APPLY TO YOUR LIFE........ WRITE IT DOWN AND LIVE

" Every tear I've ever shed was released so the pain couldn't grow any longer!"

Whoever said real men don't cry was telling a damn lie because I'm a full-grown man and I've shed countless tears! Admittedly, this was not an easy thing for me to accept at first because I allowed my ego to tell me that showing emotion was a sign of weakness. For years I dealt with pent-up aggression, hurt, pain, disappointment and discouragement because I knew of no other outlet but to be mean or to keep my emotions hidden.

I'm so glad that I was able to come to a place in my adult years where I approached all of my demons and dealt with them, each and every one, so that I could release them and free myself of the hold they had on me. Before I did that my soul was being eaten away at its core and I was dying a very slow and painful death. I was so unhappy.

I wore a frown on my face for so many years that I have a permanent crease in my forehead that proves it. Every day when I look in the mirror that crease reminds me that so many years of keeping everything bottled up had beaten my spirit and turned me in to a person that I really didn't like.

I'm much happier with my life these days because I realized that it's OK to cry and release those toxic burdens that we all bear and although this crease still remains embedded on my forehead, I'm totally free from what caused it. I'm a man and it's OK to shed my tears just like it's OK for you to shed yours. You not only help yourself, you also help those care about you most. A young fool becomes an old fool if he refuses to change. When will your "foolishness" stop?

APPLY TO YOUR LIFE........ WRITE IT DOWN AND LIVE

"The day will come when you will finally pull up the anchors so that you will be able to see the shore from the sea!"

Why are you waiting to be successful? Why are you waiting for someone else to give you something in order to begin your journey to success? Why are you sitting on your God-given talent(s) because you are afraid to fail?

These were all questions I'd ask myself during my climb. I was guilty of these things early on in my life and career because I somehow felt it SHOULD be easy…..SOMEONE was going to GIVE me my success…..MAYBE I SHOULDN'T take this chance. I WAS ONCE AFRAID to take those chances and just wait for someone else to acknowledge that I exist.

Boy, was I wrong and naïve! After some soul searching and LIVING in our beautiful but cruel world I realized that I WAS RESPONSIBLE FOR MY WELL-BEING and MY HAPPINESS. If it was success that I wanted it was going to be up to me to create the plan to go out and get it. I'm not saying that you won't need some help along the way to get your ship sailing, but I am saying you better get busy BUIDING YOUR OWN SHIP because others are going to sail with or without you.

Are you going to be the own captain of your vessel or will you be waving from the shore, watching as someone else's ship grows smaller in the distance because you've been left behind? Sometimes we pour cement on our own feet without even realizing it, anchoring ourselves, because we get so comfortable standing safely on the shore. THE SHORE is for ORDINARY PEOPLE. WHY SETTLE FOR BEING ORDINARY?

Pick up that damn anchor and sail. There's a whole world out there that's filled with amazing experiences. Set sail and try to conquer all of them!

APPLY TO YOUR LIFE.........WRITE IT DOWN AND LIVE

" Be useful to the world and human kind, and just give a damn about it!"

I truly believe that, as a society, we can reach our greatest potential if we loved more, respected more and accepted the fact that, though there will always be differences among people, those differences don't have to segregate and separate us.

Maybe I'm a little naive when it comes to this but I do look forward to a day when we put an end to all of the hate and dissention toward one another, and find a way to live with one another so that we can truly enjoy our very short time on this earth.

The kind of hatred that is spawned by racial, religious, gender and socioeconomic disparities was here long before any of us was even born; and maybe we are already behind the eight ball, but I do dream that for one day…just one day….there could be no terrorism, no racism, and no political or religious conflicts. All of humanity would get along and mankind would just agree that the well-being of the whole is more important than our individual agendas.

Sounds crazy, right? But what is even crazier is the fact that this is a wish that I know will never be more than that: a wish. The kind of world we live in is angry and hostile…and that's scary. I'm afraid, not only for my generation, but for my young son's generation as well because the state of the world gets worse as the years go by. People seem to no longer value human life and are not afraid to end it, others' or even their own.

The senseless violence has to stop and, although it may be a lofty goal, I will continue to do my part in the uplift of all people and connect the borders that divide us…simply because I give a damn!

APPLY TO YOUR LIFE........WRITE IT DOWN AND LIVE

" Self-motivation is a characteristic that can never be seen as flawed!"

We as humans will have many characteristics that might be seen as flawed, and sometimes the flaws in us may be very real. But, I will guarantee you this: that one called self-motivation will never be one of them.

So many people in society are paying someone else to tell them what to do, how to live and when to make life-changing decisions. Hey, if you need that type of push and have the finances to pay to have your life micromanaged in that way, then, go ahead, by all means, let someone else be your guide. But there is something fascinating about being your own motivator. There is something valuable about being able to test yourself and push your own buttons to reach your desired goals and even your limitations.

Every day I motivate myself because I still want so much more out of life. I use anything and everything as motivation to give me that push to go farther, even when I feel like I can't take another step. My biggest motivator, though, is my son. Every time I look at him or hear him call me "Daddy" it lights a fire within me and I know I have to go out and tackle this world to try and make it better for him. Sometimes that may require me to be away from him, which kills me, but the motivation to make his life better keeps me focused on achieving every goal I set for myself.

Making my mother proud of me is also a motivational push. There is nothing like hearing your mother brag about how well her sons are doing or what upstanding people they are. To be one of the reasons my mother smiles is another reason why I push myself so hard.

So, in the simplest terms, the hunger for a better life for me and the people I love most motivates me. No matter how successful they are, everybody that I know wants to do better today than they did yesterday, and if that desire is not the source of your motivation, then you're simply not cut from the same cloth that true winners are. You have to have reasons to get up and make things happen in your life. Remember, in the end, it's solely up to you to get everything you feel you need and want in life. Motivate yourself and obtain!

APPLY TO YOUR LIFE.........WRITE IT DOWN AND LIVE

"If you keep hitting dead ends, then it's because you refuse to abandon that road that is constantly leading you to nowhere!"

Not only is this relatable when it comes to your profession, it also rings true for personal relationships. Too many times we are traveling on a dead-end road, expecting that hopeless situation to change. We become so engrossed in making it through those seemingly endless "bad times" that we forget to look at the warning signs on the side of the road that are telling us to "detour" or even "turn around."

How do you expect to arrive at a different destination when you continue to stay on the same road? Your internal GPS constantly gives you alternative routes, some are even shorter and less-travelled, but you still convince yourself that it's better to go with the route you're used to because it is familiar; and you end up enduring the pain of failure over and over again, rather than step out on faith and try to go another way. So, what eventually ends up happening? You get the same result every time!

Some people are gluttons for punishment and I know I'm guilty of this. I was hard-headed and didn't want to heed anyone's attempts to help me. I thought that I could do it all by myself and travel my route without any guidance until I stopped and realized that I wasn't walking alone. My navigation system was my faith. God was walking with me and sometimes carrying me over the obstacles that not even I could see. Imagine how much easier and smoother my travels could have been if I had realized this earlier in my life and simply followed the inner voice of God as he spoke to me.

We are so hard on ourselves when it comes to trusting God and the inner voice that He has given us. We tend not to take our own advice or we refuse to listen to the spiritual advice that we seek. Why ask questions when you ignore the answers that are set before you? A warning sign is just that: a *warning*. So why not take heed, abandon that old route and try a new one? Stop heading down roads you know lead to nowhere. Be courageous enough to LISTEN to your inner GPS: God's Prayerful Spirit. It will never steer you wrong!

APPLY TO YOUR LIFE........ WRITE IT DOWN AND LIVE

"Faith works better for those who question it less and practice it more!"

I could write a novel on this because I have failed many times in my life when it came to questioning my faith. It is so very easy when things are going wrong to ask, "Why me?" It is a fair question and many, if not all, of us will come to this point and we will definitely NOT be thinking about faith when it happens.

We are so busy trying to get through the issue at hand that we fail to forget that if we just had a mustard seed of faith then our burdens could be a bit lighter. As humans, we naturally take on the weight of the world and try to FIX what ails us but I'VE LEARNED through my own trials and tribulations that I cannot do it all by myself. I NEED HELP. I NEED GUIDANCE. I NEED SOMEONE to speak to my soul and carry me when I don't feel like I can walk any further. I turn to my FAITH every chance that I get because God is the only one who LISTENS without judgment or ridicule. My faith also gives me a sense of safety and peace when my journey becomes filled with turmoil.

Pray to your God. Exercise your faith with Him and allow those burdens to be drowned by the resurgence of full-fledged faith healing. I will not sit here and write that I pray every day or that I don't still question my faith at times because I'd be lying. I will say that I KNOW that having FAITH has healed me from a place where I never felt secure. Now I can navigate life's twists and turns so much better; knowing that somehow, in some way everything is going to be all right; and I don't have to see the path before me to know that it will lead me to where I should be!

APPLY TO YOUR LIFE........WRITE IT DOWN AND LIVE

"There is no secret to success. Taking chances on your success is the key for everyone!"

Everyone who is successful was not born with a silver spoon in their mouths or with the advantages of wealth and prosperity. Most of us had to work extremely hard to obtain everything we have, but the one thing that we all share is that we can all have our own share of success if we are willing to take the necessary risks to be successful.

I have become a MASTER at taking chances and betting on me. I think it derives from me believing that ANYTHING is possible. I understand that privilege is not for everyone, but if you play it safe when it comes to your success, then you may be selling yourself short. My philosophy is, "If you're already down and out, what exactly are you afraid to lose?"

I may be much more of a daredevil than the average person because a lot of my moves are highly calculated. Not in the sense that I have already thought out the outcome; more so that, before I even start, I've already told myself there's not much worse that can happen to me if I don't take a chance.

SUCCESS is for anyone who seeks it, but there's no BLUEPRINT for it. You have to go out, roll up your sleeves, toughen your skin and hit the pavement with malicious intent to get everything you feel you deserve. The most successful people in our history came from nothing, but they all shared one thing: THEY BELIEVED DEEP DOWN THAT THEY WERE DESTINED TO DO GREAT THINGS!

APPLY TO YOUR LIFE........WRITE IT DOWN AND LIVE

"IF YOU ARE LOOKING INTO THE MIRROR AND YOU DON'T LIKE THE IMAGE THAT IS STARING BACK AT YOU, CHANGING THE MIRROR WON'T FIX THE PROBLEM!"

I suffered from this "SICKNESS" for many of years. Those on the outside looking in wouldn't have known this because I was very good at masking my hurt; but deep down inside, I wasn't happy with the person I was. I had some internal issues that needed to be addressed, and before I made the decision to "help" myself, I painted a picture of contentment that I knew was fooling everyone.

The image I portrayed was NOTHING like the man I saw in the mirror every day. I was even foolish enough to think I could get away with not being ME. But when I decided to stop feeling sorry for myself and chose to like me, I was able to BREAK the mirror that captured the pitiful image and replace it with one that truly reflects who I am. As a result, my present became much clearer and my future became even brighter.

I knew that nothing good was going to come from my refusal to change, and I got tired of blaming everyone else who had absolutely nothing to do with my self-reflection. Too many years are wasted in this life when you constantly run from self-reflection because, no matter how much you try, you will NEVER be able to run from the truth…whatever it is. REFUSE to have self-hatred and uplift yourself by allowing your spirit to manifest in the boldness of what it is meant to be. And, never forget that as the IMAGE changes, so does the MIRROR that captures it.

APPLY TO YOUR LIFE........ WRITE IT DOWN AND LIVE

" In the attempt to do what is right, some things will SEEM wrong."

I have found myself in this position many times. The best example that I can give that applies to my life is my pursuits in acting. NOBODY can question the love that I have for my profession and my desire to be one of the very best at it. I have sacrificed some major things in my world that have caused more pain than I would like to admit.

As an actor, one will go many years without having the security of what a corporate nine-to-five can offer. It's not only hard to maintain your sensibilities; it's hard to maintain a healthy personal life, too. My personal life has been affected for more than twenty years because I KNOW my pursuits in entertainment will be better for me in the long run as opposed to something else I could have easily chosen because it was "safe."

Some people might see this situation as WRONG because of the other responsibilities that should take precedence. Some may even be right in thinking that but I believe that the profession I have chosen will serve me in taking care of my responsibilities better in the larger scheme of things because it will give me the options to provide for those I love without the fear that it could all be taken away.

MY gamble and MY belief have caused turmoil and a loss of friends, family and loved ones who saw my plan DIFFERENTLY. They didn't see that, ultimately, whether I win or lose, it is my decision to benefit from or lose with.

You may be faced with a problem like this that could cause you to question your path, but don't panic. THAT'S NATURAL. THAT'S HUMAN. You might even think you're wrong and feel guilty for your decision(s), but you have to keep pushing because that inner voice doesn't lie. You need to listen to what it is saying.

I'm being a good listener when it comes to my prosperity, and if it takes me losing certain people along the way, then so be it. But when it all begins to make sense, my "PRIORITIES" will appreciate my decision to think about THE BIGGER PICTURE.

"Sometimes you have to cross the line to test your resilience."

I've never been the SAFE guy. I've never been the guy who didn't gamble or take chances because I didn't see the reward in playing it close. Many of the most influential people in the world took major chances in order to get where they are, and I'm sure many failed many times but they continued to move on and dared to cross that line because they knew they were onto something.

I must confess, I'm a HABITUAL LINE-CROSSER because I do challenge authority at times. Who's to say what you're being told is always right? Do your research. Ask the tough questions. Know your resolve. Know who YOU are and if someone is attempting to paint you differently than you see yourself, it's up to YOU to give them a well-informed definition.

I'm not saying be ignorant, deranged or unprofessional in defining who you are or in how you approach life's situations, but I am saying be true to yourself when it comes to going after something that you clearly want. Whether it be jobs, opinions, or relationships, NEVER be afraid to cross that imaginary line and show resilience when it comes to what may be right in your eyes.

Now, being WRONG comes in a very friendly package within this equation and you have to be willing to take that pill even if water is not offered with it. The great thing about crossing that line is that more times than not you could be RIGHT and your life can change for the better. Isn't that why we are placed on this beautiful earth? We need to challenge ourselves, folks, so go out and live your dreams!

APPLY TO YOUR LIFE........WRITE IT DOWN AND LIVE

"NEVER apologize for being BOLD!"

TALK ABOUT BEING JUDGED! Oh, yes! You will be if you live boldly. I say that with a smile on my face, but I'm as serious as the day is long. Boldness can easily be mistaken for arrogance but, personally, I just don't play in to it!

When did it become wrong for someone to be CONFIDENT about themselves? When did it become passé for humans not to acknowledge the good they represent and show why it can be infectious? I've always felt it was other people's problem, NOT MINE, if they had an issue with me being bold because I am secure in my own skin.

You see, most of us were born to be very coy when it came to compliments from others, as if their opinion about you was some sort of gift, and we should remain docile while accepting it. I did that when I didn't know any better, but now I own my boldness. I must admit that my boldness has gotten me a lot farther faster than it did when I was trying to mask it; back when I CARED what others may have thought if I told them I ALREADY KNEW I was pretty awesome or GOOD at what I did. YOU WILL FAIL everyday trying to please the masses as MANY of them will have a negative opinion of you no matter what you do.

LIVE YOUR LIFE to be heard, and if being BOLD causes other people to become uncomfortable, SIT BACK AND WATCH THEM SQUIRM! BE WHO YOU ARE and don't apologize for it!

APPLY TO YOUR LIFE........ WRITE IT DOWN AND LIVE

"I've been told many times I have a strong personality and an intimidating presence, but I quickly understood that that was not MY problem."

I laugh as I write this because earlier in my career I remember two occasions where I was up for very good roles and the casting directors looked me in the eye and, before I even uttered a word, said, " You have a very intimidating presence about you."

I knew right then that the road to conquering Hollywood was going to be a long one for me. I knew then that I would have to be a PROFESSIONAL SMILER in order to make others feel safe about THEIR insecurities. I have opinions about many things but I usually don't share them, especially in show business, because that can result in never, ever working again because the people who make the biggest decisions tend to have the thinnest skin when you show the kind of strong personality that may not be considered the norm.

By no means am I saying be an arrogant ass and purposely go into a situation looking to make others uncomfortable, but what I am saying is that there will be people in your life who will not be able to accept the strong presence and personality you may wear on your sleeve.

I didn't get those jobs and I'm not saying it was because of the things that were pointed out. Heck, it could have been that I did a poor job in my auditions or at matching up when it came to the bigger names who were vying for the same roles. But I can assure you of this: my commanding presence was felt and has been called out many times since then.

You can make adjustments in life and situations but ultimately when you look into that mirror, YOU ARE WHO YOU ARE and whoever you may be dealing with will have to take it or leave it. Just know that that door swings both ways: confidence and inner strength can be a gift and a curse.

APPLY TO YOUR LIFE.........WRITE IT DOWN AND LIVE

"When you give the universe "good," she will respond with BLESSINGS."

I'm yelling this at the top of my lungs: "IF YOU PUT GOOD ENERGY OUT, GOOD ENERGY WILL RESPOND BACK with a HELLO AND THANK YOU FOR DOING ME WELL!"

I learned this many years ago as I saw my great-grandmother do this for everyone she came across. She didn't have much in terms of money, but her LIFE was a BLESSING and the lessons she taught younger generations were PRICELESS. There wasn't a soul around who didn't want to do for "Momma." She was loved and adored by all who came in contact with her and I took notice.

When going through hard times, it can be very difficult to think about the universe and "energy," especially when you're suffering. I have been guilty of that while navigating through rough times but, I swear, when I decided to say, "Damn this. I have to make changes and just try putting more good out like "Momma" used to do," I saw a huge difference in the direction of my life.

My goodness! It made such a positive difference in my life. I have the greatest supporters and followers who have helped me throughout my life. Some of these people have never met me, personally, but have felt my energy through a quote or acknowledgement on my networks and reached out to me to say, "THANK YOU. I NEEDED THAT TODAY!"

I really get a kick out of that because, in some little way, I'M HELPING SOMEONE other than myself and I guess that was the underlying lesson that "Momma" was trying to teach those who came across her angelic presence: Remove your selfishness for just a minute and put out the GOOD ENERGY that someone else needs and watch YOUR needs be met by that same energy.

Thanks to all who have received my energy with an open heart and a loving spirit. In turn, I wear yours as a badge of honor and with the utmost respect. You have gotten me through some very hard times and made me smile when I didn't want to.

It's not hard to engage someone by saying, "Are you OK;" "Do you need anything;" "Just thinking about you;" "Has anyone ever told you that you were beautiful;" or, just a simple "Hello;" or "Have a wonderful day." I do my best to do these things on a daily basis and many of you who know me can attest to this. There isn't a woman I could come across that I won't give a true and sincere compliment to, no strings attached. I do this because: 1) it's the truth; and, 2) every woman needs to hear how truly special she is.

So, good energy is my drug of choice and I don't mind sharing it. I advise each of you to get a dose of it and see how much it changes your life!

APPLY TO YOUR LIFE........WRITE IT DOWN AND LIVE

" Stop making excuses for why you are not where you want to be in life!"

YOU are responsible for YOU. Nobody owes you anything. We all may not receive the same tools to gain success, but we all have a chance to be successful.

If you are unhappy with your job, DO WHAT YOU NEED TO DO TO FIND ANOTHER ONE. If you need or want more education, GO BACK TO SCHOOL. If you want to be a better spouse/friend/partner, BE THAT by doing what is necessary to honor those relationships that are most important to you. If you are tired of being locked up and/or having a record where nobody wants to hire you, trust you or deal with you, then STOP LIVING, THINKING AND ACTING WITH THE INCARCERATED MENTALITY that will ultimately lead you back to jail.

Life is really much simpler than we want to admit. It's easier to do the right things to position yourself to be prosperous than it is to do wrong and reassure yourself by making an excuse for why you lose. Most times we put ourselves in situations that we already know will lead to a negative outcome, but we do it anyway. WHY? Because we refuse to see that the easy way is usually not worth the price we'll have to pay once we get caught taking the shortcut.

I got tired of getting the shaft and making excuses, so I finally decided to remove the excuses from my life and take responsibility for my own actions, or lack thereof. I'm glad I did because excuses truly lead you nowhere.

Do you know where you are going?

"Sometimes you have to fall and lose it all to see where you should be headed."

I've had it all and lost it all. There will be times in life where you forget that you can lose everything at the drop of a dime. There will be times in life when you won't appreciate the little things you have or the blessings that were bestowed upon you…until it's all gone.

I've been in this situation a time or two, but it wasn't because I wasn't appreciative or I refused to see the blessing. My problem was that I thought times would always be good. I forgot about the circumstances that could arise to remove the noise of success and force me to be silent long enough to listen to God's true plan for my life. That was the moment that I knew I needed to regroup.

I had to acknowledge that even the best fall down. But what do you do when YOUR fall comes? Do you stay down?…Complain?…Cry?…yelling, "Woe is me?" You can do all of that. I know I did. But hell, I got tired of hearing my own sorrowful voice and decided to get up and brush myself off. Those times of loss gave me a new perspective and forced me to direct my life into a new space. It gave me a keener resolve and a different purpose for how I should see my blessings. It forced me to consider WHY I was blessed as opposed to HOW MUCH I was blessed with. Everything is beautiful when the sun is shining, but what happens when the forecast remains stormy with no sun in sight? Change your OUTLOOK and it may change your OUTCOME.

APPLY TO YOUR LIFE........WRITE IT DOWN AND LIVE

"By day's end, I've quit a million times in my mind; but by the next morning, I've always found one more reason carry on!"

First let me say that my problems are no bigger than anyone else's; neither is my struggle. I've wanted to give up and quit so many times simply because I was just tired of being tired. It's so easy to quit and give up when things aren't going your way. We all have had those days where we wanted to pull our hair out, as well as those days when it was all lovely. I've had days when I just wanted to end it all because nothing was going right with my career or my relationships, no matter how much I tried. I knew there had to be a better way; a way that didn't hurt as much, a way that didn't make you want to scream at the top of your lungs, "HELP ME, DAMMIT! I CANT DO THIS ALONE!"

Every one of those nights, I said, "F*@K IT! THAT'S IT! I'M DONE!" But when I woke the next morning, I'd say to myself, "JAH gave me another day to get this right!" Too many of us make permanent decisions based on temporary problems because we fail to understand that life is a marathon and not a sprint.

I'm no different than you are, but I choose to believe that the day you decide to quit may be the day before it's your turn. YOUR MOMENT may be right around the corner. You never know when your time will arrive, so don't be so quick to give up when things don't happen for you right away. As crazy as this may seem because I've accomplished so much, I'M STILL WAITING for my moment…my around-the-corner, big win…and this will be my twenty-third year standing in line. How long have you been waiting?

APPLY TO YOUR LIFE........WRITE IT DOWN AND LIVE

"Everyone has "behind-the-scenes" moments but the world only gets to see the final picture."

Some of you have seen me on television and award shows, in movies or theatrical plays, or at book signings. Some of you have even heard me in radio interviews…all smiles seeming like I had no worries in the world. WRONG, ALL WRONG! You're only seeing the product of the pain I've had, and still have, to endure to be successful.

None of you saw the tears I've cried when things weren't going right. None of you felt the pain when I had zero dollars in my account and bills to pay. None of you heard the arguments with my loved ones who didn't understand my life and what I was trying to do. None of you heard the words, "I JUST CAN'T BELIVE IN YOUR DREAMS ANYMORE. FIND SOMETHING MORE REALISTIC!" None of you heard my son say, "DADDY, I MISS YOU. I WANT TO COME WHERE YOU ARE." None of you knew that when I had no money and no place to go, I slept on couches and in vehicles until the money came through to remove me from those situations.

You see, all the good things people see about my life, and even yours, are just the smoke in a mirror that has been broken time and time again. Reality affects everyone and we are all one day from either being a millionaire or a vagrant on the street.

Life is REAL. It's not scripted, nor is it easy. So, the next time you find yourself saying, "I wish I had his/her life," make sure you consider all that the other person must endure to live that life; how much is real and how much is smoke and mirrors. I can assure you that the reality may change how you see them or make you respect the hustle that made them who they are.

I appreciate every hardship; every rough, "behind-the-scenes" moment that I've had, and every one that is to come, because I know that with my faith and my resilience I'LL BE ALL RIGHT.

APPLY TO YOUR LIFE........WRITE IT DOWN AND LIVE

"I'm very aware that racism exists. I just choose not to be a part of spreading the epidemic of ignorance!"

This will be a very short and simple "ISM" and how I apply it to my life. RACISM IS WRONG AND UNACCEPTABLE, both to convey and to indulge in. It's something that is TAUGHT, period.

We can all have our differences of opinions and our personal beliefs, but the color of one's skin should not spark the type of hatred that compels you to cause harm to someone else. I DON'T CONDONE RACISM, nor do I want to be associated with ANYONE who may practice it.

I refuse to continue to spread this sickness and its ignorance to my child but I'm also a responsible parent and a realist. It is my duty to teach him about the world we live in. I would be remiss if I didn't prepare him with the knowledge that he will have to endure the plague of racism; but at the same time, I must temper those lessons with the instruction to NEVER PERPETUATE IT.

Don't be the person who teaches your child about race relations from a perspective of hatred. Racism is ignorant in ALL forms and I refuse to add more fuel to the fire that already burns around it. We have children to raise, so let's give them a chance to succeed where previous generations have clearly failed. We must be the generation that attempts to make the change toward positive race relations.

"Disappointment has no friends, but keeps many enemies!"

Disappointment will eventually visit everyone which will cause us to hate its arrival every single time. There's no protection from it, nor is there any medication to you can take once it makes you sick. Time is the only cure for disappointment and time will only give you a reprieve until the next time disappointment arrives.

Oh, yes. It comes when it wants to, and it usually comes unannounced. You'll never be prepared for it. Isn't that something else? Disappointment will cause you to lose sleep, hair, patience and maybe even your mind. It doesn't care about gender, socioeconomic status, race, creed or color. It is an equal-opportunity burden of life…and I hate it. It is CLEARLY my enemy! Every time I think I'm about to get a breather from it, DISAPPOINTMENT knocks on my door to make sure I haven't become too comfortable.

Oh, you thought it only happens to you? You thought you were the only one being picked on? Ha! One thing we ALL have in common is this: we share the enemy, Disappointment, and though it may sometimes teach us great lessons, it will never be our friend!

"The things I was once most afraid of were the things MY EGO was telling me I SHOULD be because FAILURE could be an option."

Do you know that your ego can work against you? Yes, the same ego that causes you to walk around with your chest out; the same ego that makes you boldly voice opinions and even cause you to lose out on HELP, can be your greatest liability. It makes you afraid that others may see your needs as weaknesses. It is the same ego that will tell you that you shouldn't do something because IT HAS A FEAR OF FAILURE.

Notice, I said "IT." Yes, the ego stands alone when it comes to decisions that you may need to make in life. Early on in my adult life, I listened to my ego far too much and it kept me from accomplishing many things because I allowed it to speak for me. I listened to everything it had to say.

Some may say, "Well I thought the ego was supposed to be bold and say the unsaid?" Yes, it is bold and yes, it causes many things but nobody told me that the ego could also drown out your most constructive thought processes. Because my ego was in a fragile state, I allowed it to tell me to walk away from ideas and possible achievements because there was a chance I would fail. My ego wasn't trying to experience failure, so it constantly told me to pass on opportunities that could have been life-changing.

Right now, I know you're saying, "Wow, that's me!" Yes, it is, and for those who let your ego speak for you, you may miss out on what fear is telling the ego to pass on. Be FEARLESS and tell your ego to stay in its place because, many times, it may be hindering your growth…and your success.

APPLY TO YOUR LIFE........WRITE IT DOWN AND LIVE

"A smiling face has a way of despising what's attempting to suppress it!"

How many times have you had a horrible day at work?...Somebody has really gotten under your skin?...Your kids are messing up in school and you just are not having a pleasant day? Then, out of the blue, someone gives you a big smile and says, "Hello;" "Have a wonderful day;" or, "It's going to be OK."

This happens to me all the time. Smiles have an effect on a person that is much stronger than you could ever imagine. A smile can almost make you forget what ails you. Maybe it's the genuine place from which it derives. Maybe it's attached to a beautifully-spirited person. Maybe it's in the form of a funny joke. Whatever its source, we need to utilize and share smiles more often because sometimes it takes just that small gesture to change the direction of someone's day.

I can remember about fifteen years ago, I was sitting in a doctor's office waiting for a routine checkup. I didn't have health insurance and very little money. Bills were piling up and I was just spent. An elderly woman came in with her grandchild and sat beside me. They both said hello to me and I gave a reply back. I wasn't in the mood for conversation but something kept telling me to look over at the little girl because I felt her staring. I looked over and she winked her eye. I looked away, saying to myself, "I'm not in the mood."

A few minutes passed and something told me to look again and I did. She winked again, this time with both eyes, and smiled. I looked away, still annoyed with myself and my situation. A few more minutes passed and I looked again because I could feel the stare grabbing my face and telling me to turn toward them so I did. When I looked at her, the little girl said, "You're not smiling and I've winked at you twice. If I have to wink a third time, we're going to fight!"

All I could do was burst out in laughter because she was clearly serious. She didn't even crack a smile, and to add to the story, her grandmother smiled at me and said, "Well, if you don't smile, you're already at the doctor's office so it will be a short trip when she knocks you out!"

I laughed so hard, I forgot about the fact that I was broke and had no insurance. The very next day when I checked my mail, I had ten residual checks that totaled over seven thousand dollars, and all I could remember was that little girl gave me a reason to forget all that I hadn't had the day before.

Moral: SMILE! It's infectious!

"Your heart won't survive if bombs continue to be dropped on it!"

If you have been one of the fortunate ones who has never had their heart broken at some time in your life, then please send your four-leaf clover and rabbit's foot to my PO BOX ASAP! I don't know about you, but the affairs of the heart may be the biggest issue that any of us may ever have in a short lifetime.

That's the part of us that gets hurt repeatedly but the part that we rely on most to live a full and rich life. Imagine how it must feel on a daily basis trying to keep us upright but constantly being punched, kicked, rolled over, lied to, and stepped on. The list of how much we abuse the heart could go on and on, but the responsibility it has to add value to our existence is far greater than we give it credit for.

The only thing that I can say about this is: do your duty to not hurt others because heartbreak is not only a painful experience, it's also a very painful lesson. Nobody in my past has ever told me that I broke their heart with any "bomb" that I detonated, but I do know that there was a time in my life when I was very mean-spirited. I've spoken about it in some of the "ISMS" before this. In fact, I was verbally abusive which could have caused hearts to break.

When I was able to deal with my demons, I actually reached out to all those in my past and apologized profusely to them because what I'd done to them wasn't right. That weighed so heavily on my mind that I made it my business to MAKE it right because you never know how your issues can affect someone else's life.

And, as it always does, Karma eventually came knocking on my door and bombs were dropped on my heart, too. Boy, did it hurt like hell and I just had to live with it. I say all the time, Karma caught up with me and paid me back for all the wrongs I had done in my past. Even now, I'm still in the process of healing and the Band Aids are still barely covering the deep wounds those bombs have caused. Not everyone can deal with such deep hurt. Even the heart reaches a threshold when it has had enough; and, sometimes, when it's broken time and time again, it refuses to mend.

Take it from me. BOMBS HURT.

APPLY TO YOUR LIFE........WRITE IT DOWN AND LIVE

"IF YOU are CONSTANTLY waiting with your hands out for someone to give you something, you will never have a clue about what it feels like to OFFER anything to ANYONE!"

I know so many people who are just sitting around, waiting for a handout; who refuse to do anything to help their own cause. I know people who set to inherit money and are waiting for death to come so they could cash in. Heck, I know people who are waiting for others to become successful so they can jump on that money train called "Free Ride."

There is nothing cute or fancy about these types of people. It's actually quite disappointing to know that "lazy" has no depth but limitless heights. It is even more disappointing to know that hundreds of thousands of people have these traits. Here is the kicker, let you ask them for a ride, a favor, money, conversation, etc… it's incredible the number of excuses they'll give you for why they can be of no help. They have become so used to asking and taking that their mouth can't even form the letter "O" to spell "OFFER."

I never had a problem with helping people because I knew there would come a day when I might be in need and I assumed that if others saw that I was a giving person, then they would extend their hand when I was in need.

That was a HARD LESSON learned! When I most needed help, those same people were nowhere to be found. Those are the people you think you know; the people you've broken bread with, you've spent time around and who know you that seem to disappear like smoke in the wind when it's time to help someone else. They were never those who offered help. They were always the takers. But, alas, you're wasting your time being disappointed in folks like that. They have shown you who they are, and you have to respect that and appreciate that they are only doing you a favor by showing their true colors.

STRANGERS will help you faster than some family and friends when you are truly in need. I'm not saying that someone is supposed to help you every time you're in need, but what I am saying is that you should do for self AND be willing to help others. The circle does come full in life and, at any time, you may find yourself in either position, either where the circle starts or where it ends. GIVE so that you can RECEIVE, and RECEIVE knowing that you have GIVEN with the best of intentions and NOT with the greatest of expectations!

"When you lose sleep over things that you cannot control, you're just losing sleep!"

Raising my hand I'M GULITY! I have lost countless hours of GOOD SLEEP because I was worried about things that I had no control over. It's easier said than done when it comes to NOT worrying because normally, most of us are "fixers" by nature. But, the reality is this: WE DON'T ALWAYS HAVE THE ANSWERS TO FIX THE PROBLEMS OF THE WORLD OR EVEN THE PROBLEMS IN OUR LIVES!

While we're tossing and turning with frustration, the people and things we cannot change are resting peacefully. They're not worrying about how we will diffuse the bomb that's about to drop on us or how we can decipher its reasons for being involved with our life. They don't care about our feelings nor do they give a damn about our sleep patterns. So ask yourself, "Why am I giving these things so much power over me? Why is my mind in a state of chaos when, truly, there is nothing I can do to stop what's going to happen anyway?"

What I've learned to do is to JUST PRAY for the best and do my best to rest easily. I resolve to deal with the issue at hand in the morning because I REFUSE to lose precious sleep, or my even more precious sanity, over the Powers that are bigger than I am. I think you should do the same.

APPLY TO YOUR LIFE........WRITE IT DOWN AND LIVE

*"The days of wishing it was all so simple ended when you
learned the definition of 'responsibility'!"*

When I look at my son running around, laughing,
looking at movies, playing games with all of his toys and
gadgets, I can't help but to be envious of him. He has no
idea that these are the days he should cherish most
because when responsibility hits, these totally carefree
moments will come to a slow, grinding halt.

My days of wishing it was all so simple ended the day I
realized that my FATHER was NEVER going to be my
DAD. On that day, my responsibilities began. I was far
too young to even know the nuances of such a huge
word but I knew I had to learn quickly if I wanted to
survive on the mean streets called REALITY.

The childhood my son has is truly amazing. His mother is
doing an outstanding job in the raising of our PRINCE
while I'm away on the road for months at a time. It
reminds me of the days when my own mother would do
all she could to take care of HER RESPONSIBILITES: me
and my younger brother. Life wasn't much fun back
then, nor was it easy. The lack of a FATHER resulted in
me having to fend for myself when it came to knowing
WHAT and HOW a MAN was supposed to be; in essence,
putting the responsibilities of a man in the hands of a
child. Some of you may be able to relate to this "ISM"
because I AM YOU.

Responsibilities take away those sweet, simple days when everything is carefree, so go and watch your children as they play and smile because their time right now is pure and because the day will come when responsibility will change how they see the world, whether they are ready for it or not.

APPLY TO YOUR LIFE........WRITE IT DOWN AND LIVE

"Believe in yourself so much that it becomes INFECTIOUS and others will want to stand in line hoping to catch 'it'!"

It is my desire to infect everyone that I come across with the highest level of that "disease" called self-confidence. CONFIDENCE should NEVER be in short supply when it comes to posturing.

When you display confidence, people will listen, support and even envy you because not many are born to be LEADERS. LEADERS NEVER FOLLOW, and having that strong belief in you and anything that you stand for is admirable Even as a young child my self-esteem was stronger than most my age because I saw how people reacted to me and the air of dependability that I conveyed. Adults took me more seriously than those who didn't display strength or boldness. So, to this day, I do my best to never waver in my confidence because it's a standard that I set and that nobody else can define for me.

Confidence and self-esteem are innate. YOU determine your own level of each. Therefore, have the power to walk into a room and allow those who are there to consume your energy and want to know who you are. NEVER apologize for having a high level of confidence because once you allow someone to chip away at it, you will have lost control FOREVER.

APPLY TO YOUR LIFE........WRITE IT DOWN AND LIVE

"Greatness is maximizing everything you have until it bursts wide open in the form of SUCCESS!"

We all may have circumstances in life that affect the direction we are attempting to go, but there is one thing for sure: WE ALL HAVE A CHOICE TO BE GREAT in whatever we choose to do. You cannot allow the bumps in the road to change your travel. You should MAXIMIZE those bumps and allow your navigation to redirect you so that your destination remains the same.

You may hear me using the word "great" a lot. I'm fixated on it because everything that I do in life is because I'm trying to reach the goal of true greatness. I'm taking advantage of every stone that I'm turning, every road I'm traveling, and every person that I meet who may be doing something that I can learn from. I'm maximizing my moments and soaking up all the knowledge I can so that greatness will never be as farfetched and out of reach as some may try and tell you it is.

An older gentleman once told me, 'If you keep doing something long enough, you are bound to get exactly what you desire;" and, to this day, I still remember what I saw when he looked me in my eyes and I told him, "I think I have what it takes to make it."

Whether it be your profession, your relationship, or your role as a parent, you should ALWAYS strive to MAXIMIZE your opportunities to be great because, at the end of the road less traveled, there is a burst of sunshine called "SUCCESS" and it is truly for ANYBODY who wants to know what it feels like.

Stop using the excuse, "I'm a product of my environment!" I know plenty of doctors, lawyers, congressmen, professional athletes, entertainers, teachers, and even CEOs who overcame terrible hardships and disadvantages to become GREAT and SUCCESSFUL. So, what is your excuse again?

"The last person who told me I COULDN'T do something was also the first person to ask me how they could do the same thing!"

Now this is probably the funniest Kayneism to date because, if I had a dollar for every time someone has tried to tell me how I could do what I was already doing better, I'd be a multimillionaire. I'm still trying to figure out what gives a person the unmitigated gall to offer such advice when their choices have been subpar.

These are the same people who never had a dream but can surely give you pointers on how you can do better in living yours. Then you have the naysayers who will look you in your face and tell you what you won't be able to do because the box in which they reside has never had any windows.

You're probably smiling and saying, "Yes, I have those same kinds of people telling me the same thing!" They exist by the thousands and they will do whatever it takes to derail you. Here's my advice to you for these dark clouds, dream stealers and non-motivational mourners: Rid yourself of them. Don't allow them to stifle your creative juices with their wet-blanket mentalities because, nine times out of ten, they wish that they could have been so bold as to think outside of their box and believe in themselves enough to accomplish any goal.

How can they have the audacity to tell you about what you have already set in motion while they remain stuck in the rut that is their miserable lives? Adding insult to injury, after they've had enough of seeing you blossom in your successes, they'll come to you with mock humility looking for the copy of your blueprint! To people like this, I say, "Stay in your box! I'M TOO BUSY THRIVING OUTSIDE OF MINE!"

"The CHEAPEST investment on the road to success is the one you that make in YOURSELF!"

NOBODY is going to believe in you as much as you do. Nobody else owes you anything, so why do you feel that they are wrong when they don't invest in you? Why are you waiting on someone else to give you a break?

Most folks who have already made it are really not interested in helping someone else because they are exhausted from their own fight to the top, and now they want to enjoy the fruits of their labor. That doesn't make them wrong at all but other people tend to think that it does.

Why is that? Why can't we, as individuals, just invest in ourselves and enjoy the biggest reward from that risk? You'll have no one else to blame but YOU if you pull out of your own investment or if you decide to walk away from it because times got hard. YOU will be the only one to blame.

Too many times you hear how one person's decision has affected someone else's life. Why do we give others the power to direct our lives in such a way? Excuse me for being so candid but that is the laziest and stupidest thing I've ever heard. The day I realized that I was giving up my power to choose my own destiny was the day that I became MY OWN GREATEST INVESTOR!

There is no overhead when it comes to me being my own boss. I take vacations when I want and I can never be laid off. The work is harder because each day is a new adventure as opposed to knowing what your life is going to be because someone else is in the driver's seat of your life.

I've NEVER been comfortable with someone else navigating my journey, so I took control of my vessel and became the captain of my own ship; and, if I decide at ANY TIME that I want to change direction., NOBODY can tell me that I CAN'T!

APPLY TO YOUR LIFE........WRITE IT DOWN AND LIVE

"Keep in mind that there will ALWAYS be people who are waiting for you to fail. It's not always because they want what you have. Sometimes, it's that they just don't want YOU to have it!"

If you don't already know this fact of life, you better pull up a chair right now and pay close attention. Not everyone will be your fan. Did you hear me? Most people who are calling you and checking up on you are not concerned with HOW you are doing. They're concerned with WHAT you are doing.

Envy will always have a place in our society because the crabs-in-a-barrel mentality exists. It is a sickness that so many people want to see you fail at something and speak with malice about you because of their own selfish intentions and lack of creativity. Instead of encouraging one of their own, they get more satisfaction out of trying to steal your shine or throw shade upon it.

And, get this: it's not just your enemies who have never wanted anything good for you. (Hope you are sitting down. Ready?) It's even your friends in the peanut gallery, pseudo-cheering for you and clapping their hands while inwardly gritting their teeth. Oh, and that peanut gallery can be filled with the people closest to you. Yes, even some family members can provide salt for your wounds.

I've dealt with this a lot in my life; more so from associates, and even from a few friends, but I did what any person in my position should do: I GAVE THEM MORE TO DISLIKE BY BECOMING MORE SUCCESSFUL.

You see that's the gift that keeps on giving. You want to make those who don't genuinely cheer for you uneasy because it's not your problem that they are not happy with who they are.

Most importantly, though, don't fall into that barrel with them. BE SUPPORTIVE AND ENCOURAGING to those who are always working hard to achieve a goal or who may just be getting started. The best Karma is the kind that is HELPFUL, GIVING, SUPPORTIVE and ENCOURAGING. Not everyone has the guts to go out on a limb for a dream so if you come across someone who is bold enough to try, APPLAUD them with the expectation that they WILL be as successful as they BELIEVE they can be. For those who are on the sidelines waiting for your demise, DON'T PAY THEM ANY ATTENTION. That will drive them truly CRAZY!

APPLY TO YOUR LIFE........WRITE IT DOWN AND LIVE

"Because I remain persistent, aggressive, adamant and bold, I expect nothing less than to be more successful than those who settle!"

I will never settle for just anything. I will always feel that I deserve the best in life, and nothing short of death will stop me from attempting to go after it. Your tenacity should be aggressive. Persistence should be a part of your working vocabulary. Be adamant about making sure that what you are trying to accomplish doesn't stand a chance in hell of not being within your reach.

They say there's a fine line between arrogance, cockiness and self-assurance. I say that those who said that never had any intentions of crossing the line from mediocre in to excellence. One must not worry about the opinion of others because, as you climb your ladder of success, you may step on the toes of those who are not as BOLD and FEARLESS as you are.

I, too, was coy until I realized that it didn't serve my dreams and ambitions to be that way. If your true nature is to be bold, then own it. It's OK to relish in the truth. Yes, I understand about appearing coy when receiving a compliment, but if you know that what others are saying is true, then what's wrong with boldly owning it? ABSOLUTELY NOTHING, I say.

I am like this and I will teach my son this same lesson: If YOU don't believe that YOU are of EXCELLENCE; that you EXUDE BOLDNESS and TENACITY with AGGRESSIVE PERSISTENCE; then how do you expect someone else to believe in anything that you say?

AFTERWORD

I would like to THANK each and every one of you who has purchased "KAYNESIMS of INSPIRATION." I can only hope that this book can be used as a guideline for you to create your own "ISMS" and journal your life. There is a hidden beauty in being able to write things down, and I must confess that this was some of the best therapy I could have ever received because it flushed my soul of the impurities that had been weighing me down for many years. I stunted my growth as a man and, at times, as a human, and hid behind my scars because I was afraid to TALK, EXPRESS, RELIEVE and RELIVE; but eventually I accepted my flaws and faced my adversities with BOLDNESS and finally decided that I WAS OK. Not only was this a revelation, but it was also liberating. I know that I'm good with the universe because all I want to put out is the energy that is needed to starve the negativity that the masses are being fed. The world is NOT all bad, and people are NOT all bad. I'm just attempting to be the better person on the pendulum that swings left to right in this machine called humanity.

Judgments will always have their place in the eyes of people who have no other weapon against positivity, and I can accept that. I don't have to know you personally to LOVE you. We may not ever meet but I respect you and, most of all, my mother raised me to never be selfish, so I am sharing my inspiration with you so that you may be inspired to do the same. I wish success to ALL. Tell someone you love them today, even it's only you saying it to your reflection in the mirror.

JAH Bless, Omega Kayne